Python for Non-Programmers: Building Your AI, App, and Automation Projects from Scratch

Your Complete Beginner's Guide to Python, Automation, and AI-Powered Web Apps

By Dr Israel Carlos Lomovasky

2025

Book Description

Unlock Your Future with Python, AI, and Web App Creation — No Coding Experience Needed!

Are you ready to build the future instead of just watching it happen?

Python for Non-Programmers: Building Your AI, App, and Automation Projects from Scratch
is the ultimate guide to taking charge of your creativity, career, and independence —
even if you've never written a single line of code before.

In this groundbreaking, hands-on book, you'll learn how to:

Set up Python and your first coding environment in minutes — no stress, no jargon.
Automate boring daily tasks like emails, file management, and reports.
Build your first real-world apps to solve personal and business problems.
Create smart, AI-powered tools like chatbots, sentiment analysers, and image recognizers.
Turn your Python projects into powerful, publicly available web apps anyone can access online.
Explore bonus strategies to turn your skills into freelance gigs, side income, or full-fledged businesses.

Add next-generation AI features to your apps without needing a computer science degree!

This isn't just another dry technical manual.
This is a step-by-step journey that transforms you from a tech outsider into a confident, creative, future-ready builder.

Each chapter is packed with 1-hour real-world projects, instant wins, and clear, motivating explanations —
so you're always moving forward, building actual working tools that impress yourself and others.

By the end of this book, you'll have the power to:

Launch your own AI-powered websites

Build apps that automate, create, and predict

Solve real-world problems

Monetize your ideas

And shape the future with technology — not be left behind by it

You're not just learning Python.

You're unlocking a future only limited by your imagination.

No experience? No problem. No limits.

Perfect For:

- Beginners with zero coding background

- Entrepreneurs and freelancers looking to add AI and automation to their toolkit

- Creators wanting to launch apps, tools, and side projects

- Students and career-changers aiming to break into tech

- Dreamers who are ready to become doers

Start building. Start launching. Start leading.

The future belongs to creators — and your journey starts now.

Introduction

- **Why You Don't Need to Be a Coder to Build the Future**

- **How This Book Will Change Your Life**

- **What You'll Achieve by the End**

Part I: Your Python Superpower

1. **What Is Python and Why Is It Perfect for You?**

2. **Setting Up Python in 15 Minutes or Less**

3. **First Contact: Writing and Running Your First Python Code**

4. **Speaking Python: A Simple Guide to the Language of AI**

Part II: Building Your First Apps

5. **Automate Your Boring Tasks — Emails, Files, Reports**

6. **Build Your First App: Solve a Real Problem with Python**

Part III: Adding AI Magic

7. **Adding AI Magic to Your Apps: Chatbots, Image Recognition, and More**

8. **Create a Simple Web App to Solve a Real Problem**

9. Adding AI Magic to Web Apps: Smarter Chatbots, Image Analysis, and More Online

---

Part IV: Going Public

10. Launching Your AI Apps Online: A Beginner's Guide to Hosting

---

Bonus Chapters

Bonus Chapter 1: From Apps to Business — Turning Your Projects Into Income

- Freelancing, Productizing, Teaching, Consulting, Startups

- Packaging Your Apps

- Finding Users

- Monetizing Your Work

Bonus Chapter 2: Advanced AI Tricks — Smarter Models Without Heavy Coding

- Using OpenAI, Hugging Face, DeepAI

- Connecting GPT to Your Own Apps

- Building Smarter Apps Instantly

Epilogue

Your Journey Is Just Beginning

- **From Consumer to Creator**

- **How to Keep Building**

- **Your Mission for the Future**

Special Notes

- **Throughout the book: 1-hour Real-World Projects after key chapters**

- **Hands-on Python + AI skills without heavy coding**

- **Immediate practical use cases: Automation, AI assistants, web apps, business tools**

  About the Author

Introduction: Why You Don't Need to Be a Coder to Build the Future

Imagine waking up one day and realizing that you're not just scrolling through tech news anymore —

You're **building the future** yourself.

Apps, automations, and even AI tools — all created by **you**, not by some mythical "programmers."

Sounds crazy?

It's not.

You are living in the greatest technological shift in human history.

And here's the truth nobody tells you loudly enough:

You don't need to be a coding wizard.

You don't need a computer science degree.

You don't even need to know what a 'for loop' is yet.

You just need three things:

1. A willingness to learn (you've already got that — you're here!)

2. A real-world toolkit (this book gives it to you)

3. A bit of patience to build your skills one simple project at a time.

And the best part?

Python — one of the world's most powerful and popular programming languages — is **designed to be easy**, even for absolute beginners.

It's the language behind YouTube, Netflix, NASA's rocket simulations, TikTok's AI algorithms — and starting today, it's **your** language too.

How This Book Will Change Your Life

In the next few hours, you'll start:

- Automating boring daily tasks (saving time and money)

- Building simple apps that solve real problems

- Creating your first AI-powered projects without complicated math

- Launching mini tools that could even turn into businesses

No more depending on expensive developers.

No more feeling left out of the tech revolution.

No more thinking **"this isn't for me."**

This book will **walk you step-by-step** through every concept, every tool, every project — **with no intimidating jargon.**

You'll go from zero to building **real, useful projects** faster than you ever thought possible.

A Promise Before We Begin

This is not another boring technical manual.

This is your personal crash course into **tech empowerment.**

You won't just read — **you'll build.**

You won't just build — **you'll launch.**

You won't just launch — **you'll start living like a tech creator, not a tech consumer.**

Let's begin.

Your future self will thank you.

Chapter 1: What Is Python and Why Is It Perfect for You?

1.1 Meet Python — Your New Superpower

If you could pick one tool to open doors in almost **every industry** — tech, business, healthcare, finance, entertainment —

it would be Python.

Python isn't just a programming language.
It's a **gateway to the future**.

It powers your favorite apps.
It drives the AI that recommends your next Netflix binge.
It crunches the data behind scientific breakthroughs.
It even runs parts of NASA's space missions!

And guess what?
Python was specifically designed to be simple and human-friendly.
Its creator, Guido van Rossum, once said:

"Python is an experiment in how much freedom programmers need."

Translation?
You don't need to memorize complex codes.
You don't need to be a computer geek.
You just need curiosity, and a willingness to try.

That's why Python is **the best first language** for people with no programming background.

1.2 Why Python Fits *You* Like a Glove

Here's why Python is the perfect tool for non-programmers (like you, maybe!):

| Simple to Learn | Python reads almost like English. No weird symbols, no complicated setups. | | Lightning Fast Results | You can build working projects in **hours**, not months. | | Global Demand | Python skills are valuable in **any** career — marketing, finance, health, education, business. | | Thousands of Free Tools | Libraries and frameworks make anything possible: AI, apps, websites, automation. | | Huge Community | Millions of people are ready to help you (and this book will guide you too). |

1.3 Real-World Examples: Python in Action

- **Netflix:**

  Predicts what you want to watch using AI models built with Python.

- **Instagram:**

  Python helps manage millions of daily users and massive amounts of data.

- **SpaceX:**

  Python is used for analysing data from rocket launches.

- **Healthcare:**

  AI models in Python are helping doctors predict diseases early.

- **Finance:**

  Banks use Python to automate trading, detect fraud, and build risk models.

And the best part?

You can start building your own real-world projects almost immediately.

Yes — even if you never touched code before.

1.4 What You'll Be Able to Do With Python (Sooner Than You Think)

Here's a small preview of what's waiting for you just a few chapters from now:

Create your own personal AI assistant that writes emails for you.

Automate your social media posts while you sleep.

Build a website for your business idea in an afternoon.

Write a small program that automatically tracks your expenses.

Generate business ideas, slogans, or content using AI.

Create simple automation bots that can work for you.

And trust me, **this is just the beginning.**

1.5 You vs. "The Old Way"

Let's be honest.

A few years ago, to create apps, automate businesses, or build AI tools, you needed:

- A computer science degree

- Thousands of hours of coding experience

- A team of developers

Now?

You + Python + This Book = Enough.

That's the shift happening today — a once-in-a-lifetime opportunity where **non-coders** are suddenly able to build things that **used to require an army of engineers**.

This is your time.

Let's grab it.

1.6 What's Next?

Next up:

We'll set up Python on your computer **(super fast and easy — promise)**, and you'll write your first line of Python code!

Spoiler:

It'll feel like unlocking a magic door.

Let's jump in!

(End of Chapter 1)

Quick Recap of What We Have So Far:

- **Table of Contents** (full, structured)

- **Style/Tone** (engaging, motivating, simple)

- **Introduction** (4 pages draft)

- **Chapter 1** (full detailed draft)

Chapter 2: Setting Up Python in 15 Minutes or Less

2.1 Let's Get You Ready (Super Fast)

Good news:

Setting up Python today is **way easier** than it was just a few years ago.

No confusing steps.

No strange tech jargon.

No need for any special hardware — **your regular laptop or desktop is perfect**.

By the end of this chapter, you'll have:

- Python installed

- A "code editor" ready (like Microsoft Word, but for code)

- Your very first Python program running!

Let's go.

2.2 Step 1: Install Python

What You Need:

- A Windows PC, Mac, or Linux computer

- Internet connection

- About 15 minutes (or less!)

Download and Install:

1. **Go to the Official Python Website:**

   https://www.python.org/downloads/

2. **Download the Latest Version:**

   - Click the big yellow button (it will say something like **Download Python 3.13.x**).

   - Don't worry if the version number changes — just grab the latest one!

3. **Run the Installer:**

   ○ **IMPORTANT:** Before you click "Install Now," make sure you check the box that says:

   "Add Python to PATH".

   (This makes sure your computer knows where to find Python.)

4. **Click "Install Now"** and let it do its magic.

   ○ It usually takes about 2–3 minutes.

5. **Check if It's Working:**

   ○ Once installation finishes, open a new **Command Prompt** (Windows) or **Terminal** (Mac/Linux).

   ○ Type:

   ○ python --version

   ○ Press **Enter**.

If you see something like:

Python 3.13.2

Congratulations! You've installed Python!

2.3 Step 2: Install Your Code Editor

You need a simple, free editor to write and run your Python code.

The best option?

Visual Studio Code (also called **VS Code**).

Here's how to set it up:

1. **Go to the Official VS Code Website:**

   https://code.visualstudio.com/

2. **Download the Version for Your System:**

   o   Windows, Mac, or Linux — pick yours.

3. **Install it Like Any Other App:**

   o   Just follow the on-screen instructions.

4. **(Optional but Recommended) Add the Python Extension:**

   o   Open VS Code.

   o   Go to the **Extensions** tab (it looks like four little squares on the side).

   o   Search for "**Python**."

   o   Click **Install** on the one made by Microsoft.

This extension will make writing Python even easier (color coding, error checking, and more).

2.4 Step 3: Run Your First Python Code!

Now, let's test everything — and give you your first taste of success.

Let's Do It:

1. **Open VS Code.**

2. **Create a New File:**

- o   Click **File** → **New File**.

- o   Save it as:

- o   hello.py

(Make sure it ends with **.py** — that tells your computer it's a Python file.)

3. **Type This Simple Code:**

4. print("Hello, future Python master!")

5. **Save the File.**

6. **Run It:**

  - o   Right-click inside the code editor.

  - o   Choose **"Run Python File in Terminal"** (or manually open a terminal and type python hello.py).

If you see this appear:

Hello, future Python master!

You've officially written and run your first Python program!

2.5 Troubleshooting: If Something Goes Wrong

Don't panic — small issues happen sometimes. Here's a quick guide:

Problem	Solution
Python not found	Make sure you checked "Add Python to PATH" during install. If not, reinstall.
VS Code can't find Python	Make sure the Python extension is installed. Restart VS Code after installing.
Wrong version showing	Some systems have older Python pre-installed. Make sure you run python3 instead of python if needed.

If you get stuck:

Google the exact error message — 99% of the time, someone has solved it already!

(And don't worry — this book assumes you're starting fresh and will guide you patiently.)

2.6 Quick Recap

You installed Python.

You set up Visual Studio Code.

You wrote and ran your first real program.

In less than 15 minutes, you crossed a threshold that millions of people are afraid to even approach.

You are now officially a Python user!

✋ Take a moment. This is big.

2.7 What's Next?

Now that you're all set up, we're ready to **start speaking Python**.

Next up:

 You'll learn how Python thinks — and how you can talk to it using simple, powerful commands.

You'll be writing real, useful scripts very soon.

(No complicated theory. Just building cool stuff.)

Let's keep going!

(End of Chapter 2)

Quick Update on Our Progress:

Chapter	Status
Introduction	Complete
Chapter 1: What Is Python?	Complete
Chapter 2: Setting Up Python	Complete

Chapter 3: First Contact: Writing and Running Your First Python Code

---

3.1 Welcome to Your First Real Python Adventure

You've installed Python.

You've set up your code editor.

You even ran your first simple script.

Now it's time to **really start speaking Python** —

not just copying words, but **understanding** them.

And trust me, it's easier and way more fun than you think.

In this chapter, you'll:

- Write your first *interactive* Python programs

- Learn basic building blocks of Python

- Build tiny but real mini-apps from the start

Let's make it happen!

3.2 Talking to Python: Your First Commands

In Python, **commands** are simple instructions you give to the computer.

The most basic one?

Printing something to the screen.

Example:

```
print("Hello, world!")
```

When you run this, Python will show:

Hello, world!

The print() function tells Python:

"Hey, display this for me!"

3.3 Your Turn: Mini Practice

Open VS Code.

Create a new file: first_steps.py.

Write:

```
print("Learning Python is fun!")

print("This is my first real program.")
```

```
print("I can create anything I want!")
```

Save and run it.

Congratulations, you've officially written multiple instructions in Python!

3.4 Python Syntax: Like Building Blocks

Python programs are made of small pieces that work together.

These basic building blocks are:

Block	What It Does	Example
Function	A reusable action you can call	print("Hello")
Variable	A name you give to store data	name = "Alice"
Input	Getting information from the user	input("What's your name?")
Comment	Notes inside your code (Python ignores them)	# This is a comment

---

3.5 Your First Variables: Storing Information

A **variable** is like a box where you can put some information — and use it later.

Example:

```
name = "Alice"

print(name)
```

Output:

Alice

Here:

- name is the **variable**

- "Alice" is the **data inside the box**

- print(name) tells Python to **show the box's contents**

Variables can store:

- **Text** (like names)

- **Numbers** (for math)

- **True/False** values (for decisions)

3.6 Your Turn: Mini Practice

Create a new file: my_info.py.

Write:

```
my_name = "Your Name"

my_age = 25

print("Hi, my name is", my_name)

print("I am", my_age, "years old.")
```

Save and run it.

Notice how Python **combines** text and variables inside print()?

Easy, right?

3.7 Getting Information From the User

Want to make your app **interactive**?

You can ask the user for information using input().

Example:

```
user_name = input("What's your name? ")

print("Nice to meet you,", user_name)
```

When you run this:

- Python will **pause** and wait for the user to type something.

- It will **save** what they typed into the user_name variable.

- Then it will **print** a friendly message back.

3.8 Your First Tiny App: "Hello App"

Let's combine what you just learned:

```
# hello_app.py


user_name = input("What's your name? ")

user_age = input("How old are you? ")
```

```
print("Nice to meet you,", user_name + "!")
```

```
print("Wow,", user_age, "is a great age to start coding!")
```

Run it. Interact with it.

You just made your first *real mini-app*!

3.9 Quick Recap: You Just Learned

Skill	What It Lets You Do
print()	Show information
Variables	Store information
input()	Get information from users
Comments #	Write notes for yourself

That's **the foundation** of almost every real-world program!

You're not just learning Python —

You're learning to build tools that think, react, and communicate!

3.10 What's Next?

In the next chapter, we'll level up:

 Making decisions in your code using something called **conditions**.

You'll create programs that:

- React differently based on what users type

- Make choices automatically

- Start acting "smart"!

It's going to be awesome.

Let's keep going!

(End of Chapter 3)

Quick Progress Overview

Chapter	Status
Introduction	Complete
Chapter 1: What Is Python?	Complete
Chapter 2: Setting Up Python	Complete
Chapter 3: First Contact: Writing Python Code	Complete

1-Hour Project: "Personal Budget Tracker: Your First Financial Assistant with Python"

Project Overview

We'll build a simple **Python app** where users can:

- Enter their **expenses** and **income**

- See their **current balance**

- Keep **adding entries** during the day

- Exit and save the session

Why this project?

- Everyone needs basic money management.

- Teaches loops, user input, simple calculations, file saving — foundational Python skills!

Step-by-Step Plan

Step 1: Set Up a Simple Loop for the Tracker

Create a file called:

budget_tracker.py

Start with this basic skeleton:

```python
# budget_tracker.py


balance = 0


while True:

    print("\n--- Personal Budget Tracker ---")

    print("1. Add Income")

    print("2. Add Expense")

    print("3. Show Balance")

    print("4. Exit")


    choice = input("Choose an option (1-4): ")


    if choice == "1":

        amount = float(input("Enter income amount: "))

        balance += amount

        print(f" Added ${amount:.2f} to balance.")
    elif choice == "2":

        amount = float(input("Enter expense amount: "))

        balance -= amount
```

```
    print(f" Subtracted ${amount:.2f} from balance.")

  elif choice == "3":

    print(f" Current Balance: ${balance:.2f}")

  elif choice == "4":

    print(" Exiting... Have a financially awesome day!")

    break

  else:

    print(" Invalid option. Please try again.")
```

Step 2: Test It!

Save and run the file.

You'll now have a **menu-based budget tracker** where users can:

- Add income

- Add expenses

- See their current balance

- Exit the app cleanly

Step 3: (Optional Enhancement) Save the Balance to a File

To make the data **persist** even after closing the program, let's add file saving:

Modify the code:

```python
# budget_tracker.py

import os

# Load balance if exists
if os.path.exists("balance.txt"):
    with open("balance.txt", "r") as file:
        balance = float(file.read())
else:
    balance = 0

while True:
    print("\n--- Personal Budget Tracker ---")
    print("1. Add Income")
    print("2. Add Expense")
    print("3. Show Balance")
    print("4. Exit")

    choice = input("Choose an option (1-4): ")
```

```python
    if choice == "1":

        amount = float(input("Enter income amount: "))

        balance += amount

        print(f" Added ${amount:.2f} to balance.")

    elif choice == "2":

        amount = float(input("Enter expense amount: "))

        balance -= amount

        print(f" Subtracted ${amount:.2f} from balance.")

    elif choice == "3":

        print(f" Current Balance: ${balance:.2f}")

    elif choice == "4":

        # Save balance before exiting

        with open("balance.txt", "w") as file:

            file.write(str(balance))

        print(" Balance saved. Goodbye!")

        break

    else:

        print(" Invalid option. Please try again.")
```

Now every time you exit the program, your balance is saved in a file called

balance.txt!

When you restart the app, it **loads** the previous balance automatically.

What Readers Learn from This Project

Skill	Practical Value
Loops (while True)	Keep apps running interactively
Conditionals (if/elif/else)	Make choices in the app
User Input Handling	Getting and validating user data
File Handling	Saving and loading real data
Basic Math Operations	Addition and subtraction

Real world impact:

- Building apps that **save data** = the first step toward making *real software*.

Bonus Challenges (Optional Extensions)

- **Add expense categories:** food, transport, entertainment.

- **Show expense history:** Keep a list of all entries with timestamps.

- **Add password protection:** Basic security for the budget file.

- **Visual balance warning:** Warn the user when the balance goes below $0!

Conclusion

In about 1 hour, the reader:

- Created a *working personal finance app*

- Learned loops, user-driven choices, file saving — essential Python patterns

- Built their first *"memory-enabled"* software!

Chapter 4: Speaking Python: A Simple Guide to the Language of AI

4.1 Python Is Like Speaking to a Very Smart Assistant

By now, you know how to:

- Print information

- Store information

- Get user input

- Loop through simple programs

But now we'll level up:

You'll teach Python to *think* and *make decisions*.

This is the first step toward **real AI thinking**.

Imagine this:

If it's raining, take an umbrella.

If you're hungry, make a sandwich.

That's how Python "thinks" too!

Simple **conditions** and **reactions**.

4.2 if Statements: Teaching Python to Make Decisions

The if statement tells Python:

"Only do this if a certain condition is true."

Example:

```
temperature = 30
```

```
if temperature > 25:

    print(" It's a hot day!")
```

What happens here?

- Python checks: is the temperature greater than 25?

- If yes, it prints the message.

- If not, it does nothing (for now).

4.3 else: What If the Condition Is False?

Sometimes, you want Python to **do something else** if the condition isn't true.

You use else.

Example:

```
temperature = 15
```

```
if temperature > 25:

    print(" It's a hot day!")

else:

    print(" It's a cool day.")
```

Now, Python **always does something** — depending on the situation.

4.4 elif: Multiple Choices (Like a Smart Menu)

If you have **more than two choices**, you can use elif, which means **else if**.

Example:

temperature = 5

if temperature > 25:

    print(" It's a hot day!")

elif temperature > 15:

    print(" It's a nice day.")

else:

    print(" It's cold today. Wear a jacket!")

Python checks:

1. Is it hotter than 25? If yes, do the first action.

2. If not, is it hotter than 15? If yes, do the second action.

3. If none are true Do the last option (else).

4.5 Your Turn: Mini Practice

Create a new file: weather_decision.py.

Write:

```
temperature = int(input("What is the temperature today (°C)? "))


if temperature >= 30:

    print(" It's extremely hot! Stay hydrated.")

elif temperature >= 20:

    print(" Perfect weather for a walk!")

elif temperature >= 10:

    print(" You might want a jacket.")

else:

    print(" Bundle up! It's really cold.")
```

Test it by entering different temperatures.

4.6 Making Python Repeat: Loops

Python can **repeat** actions automatically — very useful for apps that need to:

- Collect multiple inputs

- Process lists of items

- Keep running until a condition changes

There are two main types of loops:

- while loop (repeat **while** something is true)

- for loop (repeat **for each** item in a list)

4.7 while Loops: Repeat Until Something Changes

The while loop says:

*"Keep doing this **as long as** a condition is true."*

 Example:

password = ""

while password != "open_sesame":

   password = input("Enter the secret password: ")

print(" Access granted!")

- Python **keeps asking** until the correct password is entered.

- Then it moves on.

4.8 for Loops: Repeat for Each Item

The for loop says:

*"Do something once for **each item** in a collection."*

 Example:

fruits = ["apple", "banana", "cherry"]

```
for fruit in fruits:

    print("I like", fruit)
```

Output:

I like apple

I like banana

I like cherry

Simple, powerful, and very human-like!

4.9 Your Turn: Mini Practice

Create a file: favorite_things.py

Write:

```
favorites = ["pizza", "movies", "travel", "coding"]
```

```
for thing in favorites:

    print("One of my favorite things is", thing)
```

Run it — it will print your favorite things one by one.

4.10 Mixing Conditions and Loops: Power Combo!

You can even **mix if statements inside loops** to make smarter apps.

Example:

numbers = [1, 2, 3, 4, 5]

```
for number in numbers:

    if number % 2 == 0:

        print(number, "is even.")

    else:

        print(number, "is odd.")
```

Output:

1 is odd.

2 is even.

3 is odd.

4 is even.

5 is odd.

% means "remainder."

So number % 2 == 0 means "is it divisible by 2?"

4.11 Quick Recap: You Just Learned

Concept	What It Lets You Do
if/else/elif	Make decisions based on conditions
while loop	Repeat actions until something changes
for loop	Repeat actions for each item
Combining both	Build smart, dynamic apps

4.12 What's Next?

Now that you can make Python think, decide, and repeat...

You're ready to **build real-world applications** that *adapt to users*.

In the next chapter, we'll:

- Build your **first full mini-apps**

- Create fun, interactive programs you can actually **use and share**

Imagine this:

Your first *game, assistant, automator* — all from the tools you now know!

Let's keep going!

(End of Chapter 4)

Quick Progress Update

Chapter	Status
Introduction	Complete
Chapter 1: What Is Python?	Complete
Chapter 2: Setting Up Python	Complete
Chapter 3: First Contact: Writing Code	Complete
Chapter 4: Speaking Python	Complete

1-Hour Project: "Simple Python Quiz App — Test Your Knowledge!"

Project Overview

We'll build a **basic Quiz App** where:

- The app **asks multiple-choice questions**.

- The user **enters answers**.

- Python **checks correctness**.

- The final **score is displayed** at the end.

This project perfectly reinforces if/else, loops, input handling — and makes readers feel like they're building their first interactive "game" or educational app!

Step-by-Step Plan

Step 1: Set Up the Questions and Answers

We'll store questions and answers inside a simple Python dictionary:

```python
# quiz_app.py


quiz = {

    "What is the capital of France?": "a",

    "Which number is even? (a) 3 (b) 4 (c) 7": "b",

    "What is the result of 3 * 5?": "c",

    "Which language are we learning now? (a) Java (b) C++ (c) Python": "c"

}


options = {

    "What is the capital of France?": ["a) Paris", "b) Rome", "c) London"],

    "Which number is even? (a) 3 (b) 4 (c) 7": ["a) 3", "b) 4", "c) 7"],

    "What is the result of 3 * 5?": ["a) 10", "b) 12", "c) 15"],
```

"Which language are we learning now? (a) Java (b) C++ (c) Python": ["a) Java",
"b) C++", "c) Python"]

```
}
```

- quiz dictionary stores **questions and correct answers.**

- options dictionary stores **choices for each question.**

Step 2: Build the Main Quiz Logic

Now, let's create the quiz flow:

```
score = 0


for question in quiz:

    print("\n" + question)

    for option in options[question]:

        print(option)


    answer = input("Enter (a, b, or c): ").lower()


    if answer == quiz[question]:

        print(" Correct!")
```

```
        score += 1

    else:

        print(" Wrong!")


print("\n Quiz Complete!")

print(f"Your final score: {score}/{len(quiz)}")
```

- For each question:

    o Show the question and options.

    o Get the user's answer.

    o Check if it's correct.

    o Increase the score if correct.

Step 3: (Optional) Add a "Retry" Option

Want to make it replayable?

Add a simple loop around the quiz:

```
play_again = "yes"



while play_again == "yes":

    score = 0
```

```
for question in quiz:

    print("\n" + question)

    for option in options[question]:

        print(option)


        answer = input("Enter (a, b, or c): ").lower()


    if answer == quiz[question]:

        print(" Correct!")

        score += 1

    else:

        print(" Wrong!")


print("\n Quiz Complete!")

print(f"Your final score: {score}/{len(quiz)}")


play_again = input("\nDo you want to try again? (yes/no): ").lower()


print(" Thanks for playing!")
```

Now after finishing the quiz, the user can choose to **play again** or **exit**.

What Readers Learn from This Project

Skill	Practical Value
for loops	Process multiple items
if/else statements	Make decisions based on user input
Variables (score keeping)	Handling game state
Dictionaries	Managing structured data
User interaction	Building conversational apps

Bonus Challenges (Optional Extensions)

- **Add more questions dynamically**: Let users add questions.

- **Shuffle the questions**: Randomize order for replayability.

- **Multiple choice questions**: Add more options (d, e).

- **Difficulty levels**: Easy, Medium, Hard.

Conclusion

In about **one hour**, the reader:

- Created an interactive, dynamic mini-game

- Reinforced foundational Python concepts through *practical* use

- Took the first real step toward making **apps people can use and share**

Chapter 5: Automate Your Boring Tasks — Emails, Files, Reports

---

5.1 Why Automation Is the Future

Imagine:

- No more manually checking dozens of emails

- No more copy-pasting the same files every week

- No more wasting time doing repetitive reports

Automation is the **superpower of the 21st century.**

And Python makes it possible even for beginners like you.

If you can automate just 1 hour of work per day, you "create" 365 extra hours per year.

That's like getting **9 full-time work weeks for free**!

5.2 What You'll Learn in This Chapter

In this chapter, you'll create Python scripts to:

- **Send automatic emails**

- **Organize and rename files automatically**

- **Generate quick reports from data**

And you'll start to think like an *automation architect*.

5.3 Let's Start Small: Your First Automated Email

Step 1: Install the Email Library

We'll use a simple library called **yagmail**.

Install it by running:

pip install yagmail

Easy.

Step 2: Write a Simple Email Sender

Here's a super simple script:

```python
import yagmail


# Your email and app password

sender_email = "your_email@gmail.com"

app_password = "your_gmail_app_password"


# Connect to Gmail

yag = yagmail.SMTP(sender_email, app_password)


# Send an email

yag.send(

    to="receiver_email@example.com",

    subject="Hello from Python!",

    contents="This is your first automated email. "

)


print(" Email sent successfully!")
```

Important Gmail Setup Tip

Gmail doesn't allow normal password login from apps anymore.

You need to create an **App Password** (takes 2 minutes).

Go to your Google Account → Security → App Passwords → Create one → Use it here.

5.4 Next Level: Sending a Daily Report Automatically

Imagine your app sends you a **daily summary** of tasks, expenses, or reminders.

Example:

```
import yagmail

from datetime import date


# Email setup

sender_email = "your_email@gmail.com"

app_password = "your_gmail_app_password"

receiver_email = "receiver_email@example.com"


# Today's date

today = date.today()


# Message content
```

```python
message = f"Hello!\n\nHere's your quick update for {today}:\n- Tasks completed: 5\n-
Expenses logged: $50\n- Mood: Excellent "


# Send it

yag = yagmail.SMTP(sender_email, app_password)

yag.send(

    to=receiver_email,

    subject=f"Daily Update - {today}",

    contents=message

)


print(" Daily update sent!")
```

You can later automate this to run every morning using a **scheduler** (Task
Scheduler on Windows, cron on Mac/Linux).

5.5 Organizing Files Automatically with Python

Sick of messy folders?

Python can **move, rename, or organize files** while you sip your coffee.

Example: Move All .txt Files to a "TextFiles" Folder

```python
import os

import shutil


# Make sure the destination folder exists

if not os.path.exists("TextFiles"):

    os.mkdir("TextFiles")


# Scan current folder

for filename in os.listdir():

    if filename.endswith(".txt"):

        shutil.move(filename, "TextFiles")


print(" All .txt files moved!")
```

Super simple but very powerful:

- Scans current folder

- Moves all .txt files to a new folder

You can adapt this for images, videos, PDFs, anything.

5.6 Quick Mini Project: Automated Backup Script

Let's combine what you've learned:

```python
import os

import shutil

from datetime import datetime


# Create backup folder with today's date

backup_folder = f"Backup_{datetime.now().strftime('%Y-%m-%d')}"


if not os.path.exists(backup_folder):

    os.mkdir(backup_folder)


# Files to back up

files_to_backup = ["important.docx", "budget.xlsx", "notes.txt"]


for file in files_to_backup:

    if os.path.exists(file):

        shutil.copy(file, backup_folder)


print(" Backup completed!")
```

This script:

- Creates a backup folder named by today's date

- Copies selected important files into it

You just automated your own "save my important stuff" process!

5.7 Automate Your First Real-World Workflow

Here's a simple real-life workflow you can now build:

Step   Action

Morning Python sends you a daily motivational email

Noon   Python organizes downloaded files automatically

Evening Python backs up your important documents safely

This is **real automation**.

It's like having your **own personal assistant** — for free!

5.8 Quick Recap: You Just Learned

Skill   **Practical Value**

Sending emails   Automated alerts, updates, reports

Moving/renaming files Organize your digital life

Scheduling tasks   "Set and forget" productivity boosts

Backups   Protecting important data automatically

And you did it all **without writing complex code**.

Pure simple, powerful Python.

5.9 What's Next?

Now that you know how to automate simple workflows...

You're ready to **build your first full apps**!

In the next chapter, we'll move into:

- Creating **simple web apps**

- Making **your own AI-powered assistants**

- **Combining Python with web technologies**

You're stepping into the world of **real creators**.

Let's go!

(End of Chapter 5)

Quick Progress Overview

Chapter   Status

Introduction Complete

Chapter 1   Complete

Chapter	Status
Chapter 2	Complete
Chapter 3	Complete
Chapter 4	Complete
Chapter 5	Complete

Chapter 6: Build Your First App — Solve a Real Problem with Python

---

6.1 Why Building an App Is a Big Deal

You've already done small projects.

You've automated boring tasks.

Now it's time for the real magic:

- You'll solve a real problem.

- You'll create something others can actually use.

- You'll start thinking like a Python creator — not just a user.

Remember:

Big things always start with small, real-world problems.

6.2 The Simple App We'll Build: A "To-Do List Manager"

Problem:

- People often forget tasks.

- Sticky notes get lost.

- Apps like Todoist are great but sometimes you just want something simple, fast, and yours.

Solution:

- Build your own Python To-Do List App.

- Simple, fast, customizable.

Step-by-Step Plan

Step 1: App Requirements

Our To-Do App will let the user:

Add tasks

View tasks

Remove tasks

Save tasks so they persist even after closing

Load tasks automatically when restarting

Perfect for reinforcing file handling, loops, and user input!

Step 2: Start the Code

Create a file:

todo_app.py

Set up the starting point:

```python
import os


# Load existing tasks

if os.path.exists("tasks.txt"):

    with open("tasks.txt", "r") as file:

        tasks = [line.strip() for line in file.readlines()]

else:

    tasks = []


# Main loop

while True:

    print("\n--- Your To-Do List ---")
```

```python
print("1. View Tasks")

print("2. Add Task")

print("3. Remove Task")

print("4. Save and Exit")


choice = input("Choose an option (1-4): ")


if choice == "1":

    if not tasks:

        print(" No tasks yet. You're free!")

    else:

        for idx, task in enumerate(tasks, 1):

            print(f"{idx}. {task}")


elif choice == "2":

    new_task = input("Enter the new task: ")

    tasks.append(new_task)

    print(f" Added task: {new_task}")
```

```python
elif choice == "3":

    if not tasks:

        print(" No tasks to remove!")

    else:

        for idx, task in enumerate(tasks, 1):

            print(f"{idx}. {task}")

        task_num = int(input("Enter task number to remove: "))

        if 1 <= task_num <= len(tasks):

            removed = tasks.pop(task_num - 1)

            print(f"□□ Removed task: {removed}")

        else:

            print(" Invalid task number.")


elif choice == "4":

    with open("tasks.txt", "w") as file:

        for task in tasks:

            file.write(task + "\n")
```

```
print("💾 Tasks saved. Goodbye!")

    break


else:

    print(" Invalid option. Please try again.")
```

How This Works

Section	What It Does
Load tasks	Opens the existing file if there is one.
Main menu loop	Shows options and keeps the app running.
View tasks	Lists all tasks nicely numbered.
Add task	Adds a new task to the list.
Remove task	Deletes a selected task from the list.
Save and exit	Saves the tasks into a file before quitting.

Key Concepts Reinforced

- Lists (adding, removing, looping)

- File handling (read and write)

- Conditionals (if/else)

- Loops (while, for)

- User input and simple validation

These are core skills needed for much bigger apps later!

6.3 Running Your App

1. Open your terminal.

2. Navigate to the folder where your todo_app.py is located.

3. Run:

python todo_app.py

Enjoy managing your tasks like a real tech wizard.

You'll even have a "tasks.txt" file that updates automatically!

6.4 Quick Ideas to Expand Your App (Optional)

Want to make it cooler?

- Due dates: Add a deadline to each task.

- Priorities: Sort tasks by importance.

- Search function: Find tasks containing a keyword.

- Colorful output: Use colorama to color-code tasks.

(And don't worry — we'll explore this kind of expansion later in the book too.)

6.5 Quick Recap: You Just Built an App!

What You Did	Why It's Amazing
Solved a real-world problem	Practical coding
Created a working app	You're now a Python builder
Handled saving and loading data	Like real-world apps do

Made something you can actually use and share Big psychological win!

6.6 What's Next?

You've now crossed the line:

From Python beginner to Python app creator.

In the next chapter, we'll take it further:

- Build more complex apps

- Introduce AI features (yes, your apps will get "smart"!)

We're just getting warmed up.

You're on the path to tech mastery.

Let's go!

(End of Chapter 6)

Progress Update

Chapter	Status
Introduction	Complete
Chapter 1	Complete
Chapter 2	Complete
Chapter 3	Complete
Chapter 4	Complete
Chapter 5	Complete
Chapter 6	Complete

1-Hour Project: "Random Password Generator App — Create Strong Passwords Instantly"

Project Overview

We'll build a simple **Password Generator** app where:

- The user can **choose the length** of the password

- Python **randomly generates** a strong password

- The password includes **letters, numbers, and symbols**

This project reinforces randomization, loops, user input, and string manipulation — powerful real-world skills for cybersecurity basics!

Step-by-Step Plan

Step 1: Import the Needed Libraries

Start simple:

We'll use random and string, both built into Python — no need to install anything!

import random

import string

These two libraries will allow us to randomly pick characters easily.

Step 2: Write the Core Password Generator

Here's the basic script:

import random

import string

Welcome message

print(" Welcome to the Password Generator!")

Ask user for password length

length = int(input("Enter the desired password length: "))

Define possible characters

characters = string.ascii_letters + string.digits + string.punctuation

Generate password

password = ''.join(random.choice(characters) for _ in range(length))

print("\n Your generated password is:")

```
print(password)
```

- string.ascii_letters = all uppercase + lowercase letters

- string.digits = numbers 0–9

- string.punctuation = special symbols like !@#$%^&*

- random.choice() picks a random character

- ".join() glues them together into a single password string

Step 3: Add Basic Error Handling (Optional but Nice)

To make it more user-friendly:

```
import random

import string


print(" Welcome to the Password Generator!")


try:

    length = int(input("Enter the desired password length: "))

    if length < 4:

        print(" Password length should be at least 4 characters for better security.")

    else:
```

```
characters = string.ascii_letters + string.digits + string.punctuation

password = ''.join(random.choice(characters) for _ in range(length))

print("\n Your generated password is:")

    print(password)

except ValueError:

  print(" Please enter a valid number.")
```

Now if a user types "abc" instead of a number, the app won't crash — it will display a helpful message.

🔟 Bonus: How to Make It Even Cooler (Optional Challenges)

- **Allow the user to choose:**

    - Letters only

    - Letters + numbers

    - Letters + numbers + symbols

- **Add strength meter:** Rate passwords based on length and complexity.

- **Copy to clipboard:** Use pyperclip library to automatically copy password.

- **Generate multiple passwords at once:** For account managers.

What Readers Learn from This Project

Skill	Practical Value
Randomness	Randomly selecting data
Loops (for)	Create sequences of characters
String manipulation	Glue pieces together
Error handling	Build more stable apps
Security basics	Create strong, secure passwords

Conclusion

In **one hour** or less, the reader:

- Built a **real cybersecurity utility app**

- Learned important Python skills for randomness and error handling

- Created something they can **actually use immediately** (or even share with friends!)

Next Move

Now readers have:

- Built **small games**

- Built **useful automation**

- Built **file managers**

- Built **password generators**

They're absolutely **ready to step into AI territory next**!

Perfect moment for **Chapter 7**:

"Adding AI Magic to Your Apps: Chatbots, Image Recognition, and More"

1-Hour Project: "Mini Sentiment Analyser — How Positive or Negative Is Your Text?"

Project Overview

We'll build a simple app that:

- Analyses **user input** (a sentence)

- Detects if it's **positive**, **negative**, or **neutral**

- Uses **basic keyword matching** (very beginner-friendly)

This teaches real-world AI logic: text analysis, classification, simple natural language processing — but without heavy machine learning libraries yet.

Step-by-Step Plan

Step 1: Define Some Sentiment Keywords

First, create simple lists of positive and negative words:

```
# mini_sentiment_analyser.py
```

```python
positive_words = ["good", "happy", "great", "fantastic", "awesome", "amazing", "love", "excellent", "nice", "joy"]

negative_words = ["bad", "sad", "terrible", "horrible", "worst", "awful", "hate", "angry", "poor", "pain"]
```

These are simple "vocabularies" our little AI will use.

Step 2: Write the Sentiment Analysis Logic

Now build the core:

```python
def analyse_sentiment(text):
    text = text.lower()  # Make everything lowercase for easier matching

    positive_score = 0

    negative_score = 0


    words = text.split()
```

```
for word in words:

    if word in positive_words:

        positive_score += 1

    elif word in negative_words:

        negative_score += 1


    if positive_score > negative_score:

        return " Positive Sentiment"

    elif negative_score > positive_score:

        return " Negative Sentiment"

    else:

        return " Neutral Sentiment"
```

Simple rule:

- Count how many positive and negative words appear.

- Compare the scores.

- Classify the sentiment.

Step 3: Build the Main App Loop

Let's make it interactive:

```
print(" Welcome to the Mini Sentiment Analyser!")
```

```
print("Type your sentence below (or type 'exit' to quit).")


while True:

    user_input = input("\nYour sentence: ")

    if user_input.lower() == "exit":

        print(" Goodbye!")

        break


    result = analyse_sentiment(user_input)

    print("Result:", result)
```

Now users can type as many sentences as they want — and get instant feedback!

Example in Action

User types:

I am feeling amazing today! The weather is fantastic.

Output:

Positive Sentiment

User types:

This was the worst movie I've ever seen.

Output:

Negative Sentiment

User types:

I have a meeting later.

Output:

Neutral Sentiment

What Readers Learn from This Project

Skill	Practical Value
Text preprocessing	Clean and prepare text data
Basic NLP (Natural Language Processing)	Analyse and understand user language
Logic building	Score and classify based on conditions
Interactive app structure	Build "smart" chat-like applications

---

Bonus Challenges (Optional Extensions)

- **Expand the word lists:** Add more emotion vocabulary.

- **Handle typos:** Allow small spelling mistakes (using fuzzy matching).

- **Add percentage scores:** "Your sentence is 70% positive."

- **Visual feedback:** Use emoji, stars, or colored output.

Conclusion

In **less than 1 hour**, readers:

- Built a **real-world text analysis tool** 🔍

- Practiced core AI concepts like **classification and sentiment scoring**

- Created another **useful, shareable app**!

They're gaining **massive confidence** with every project.

Next Step:

Now the readers are absolutely **ready** to move into **Chapter 8**:

"Create a Simple Web App to Solve a Real Problem"

Where they'll take the apps they've built and **put them online** for others to use!

Chapter 8: Create a Simple Web App to Solve a Real Problem

8.1 Why Take Your Apps Online?

You've already built:

- Automations

- Useful desktop apps

- Mini AI tools

Now it's time to make **your apps available to others —**

accessible from any device, anywhere.

Building web apps means:

- Your projects become **real tools** that friends, clients, or users can **access online**.

- You **scale yourself** — reach more people without extra work.

- You take the first real step toward **professional software development**.

And you don't need to know complicated web coding!

Thanks to **Python libraries like Flask**, you can build web apps **super easily**.

8.2 What You'll Achieve in This Chapter

Build your first **working web app** (local version)

Learn basic **Flask** framework fundamentals

Turn any Python app into a **simple website**

Understand **how real websites work**

8.3 Meet Flask: Your New Web App Friend

Flask is a lightweight, easy-to-use web framework for Python.

Why Flask?

Reason	Why It Matters
Simple	You can build a site with just a few lines of code.
Fast	Perfect for quick projects and prototypes.
Real-world use	Companies like Netflix and Lyft have used Flask.

Good news:

Flask speaks your language — simple Python!

8.4 Setting Up Flask

Install Flask by running this command in your terminal:

pip install flask

(One of the easiest installs you'll ever do!)

8.5 Building Your First Simple Web App (Hello World)

Create a file:

app.py

Write this inside:

from flask import Flask

```python
app = Flask(__name__)


@app.route("/")

def home():

    return "<h1>Hello, World! </h1>"



if __name__ == "__main__":

    app.run(debug=True)
```

What happens here:

- Flask(__name__) creates your web app.

- @app.route("/") says: "When someone visits the homepage /, show this."

- The home() function returns a basic HTML message.

- debug=True means you'll see helpful error messages if anything goes wrong.

Run Your Web App

Open terminal, go to the folder containing app.py, and type:

```
python app.py
```

You'll see something like:

```
Running on http://127.0.0.1:5000/
```

Open your browser and visit http://127.0.0.1:5000/

You'll see: **"Hello, World! "**

You've just published your first live web page from your computer!

8.6 Turn Your Previous Projects into Web Apps

Now let's apply this to something you built —

for example, your **Mini Sentiment Analyser!**

Step 1: Set Up a New Web App for Sentiment Analysis

```python
from flask import Flask, request


app = Flask(__name__)


positive_words = ["good", "happy", "great", "fantastic", "awesome", "amazing", "love",
"excellent", "nice", "joy"]
negative_words = ["bad", "sad", "terrible", "horrible", "worst", "awful", "hate", "angry",
"poor", "pain"]


def analyse_sentiment(text):
    text = text.lower()
    positive_score = 0
```

```python
    negative_score = 0

    words = text.split()

    for word in words:
        if word in positive_words:
            positive_score += 1
        elif word in negative_words:
            negative_score += 1

    if positive_score > negative_score:
        return " Positive"
    elif negative_score > positive_score:
        return " Negative"
    else:
        return " Neutral"


@app.route("/", methods=["GET", "POST"])

def home():
    if request.method == "POST":
```

```
    text = request.form["text"]

    result = analyse_sentiment(text)

    return f"<h1>Result: {result}</h1><br><a href='/'>Analyse another</a>"

    return '''

    <form method="POST">

        <textarea name="text" rows="4" cols="50" placeholder="Type your text here..."></textarea><br><br>

        <input type="submit" value="Analyse">

    </form>

    '''



if __name__ == "__main__":

    app.run(debug=True)
```

Now:

- Users can **submit text** through a simple web form.

- Your Python app **analyses** it.

- The result is **shown instantly on a webpage**.

8.7 How This Web App Works

Part	What It Does
HTML Form	Lets user type text
POST Method	Sends the text securely to Python
Sentiment Function	Analyses the text
Web Response	Shows the sentiment result

You built a **real working AI web app** with fewer than 50 lines of Python!

8.8 Quick Ideas to Expand Your Web App

- **Make it prettier** with CSS (optional at first).

- **Allow file uploads** (analyse text from files).

- **Build login systems** (user accounts).

- **Connect to databases** (store analysis results).

We'll cover these progressively in the next sections of the book.

What Readers Have Learned in This Chapter

Skill	Practical Value
Web app basics (Flask)	Bring your apps online
HTML forms + Python	Real user interaction

Skill	Practical Value
Combining AI + Web	Real-world applications
Local hosting	Create private tools or test prototypes

Conclusion

In **one chapter**, you:

- Learned web development basics

- Built and launched your first web app

- Turned a simple Python script into a usable **online AI tool**

You're becoming unstoppable.

8.9 What's Next?

Now that you know how to build simple web apps...

You're ready to **add AI models, APIs, databases, and automation pipelines** to your apps.

Next up:

We'll learn about **adding smarter AI features** like chatbots that learn, smarter auto-categorization, even voice and image handling!

Welcome to **the creator's zone.**

(End of Chapter 8)

Progress Update

Chapter   **Status**

Introduction   Complete

Chapters 1–7   Complete

Chapter 8   Complete

1-Hour Project: "Mini AI Resume Analyser — Boost Your Job Hunt with Python"

Project Overview

We'll build a **Mini Resume Analyser** that:

- Takes **user input**: a resume text.

- **Analyses** it for key skills, experience keywords, and soft skills.

- **Gives instant feedback** on how strong the resume sounds.

- **Recommends improvements** if important elements are missing.

Teaches text analysis, keyword extraction, simple "scoring" AI techniques — highly useful for careers and freelancing!

Step-by-Step Plan

Step 1: Define Important Resume Keywords

We'll define lists for **hard skills**, **soft skills**, and **experience words**.

```python
# mini_resume_analyser.py


hard_skills = ["python", "data analysis", "machine learning", "web development",
"cloud computing", "sql", "javascript", "api", "automation", "cybersecurity"]

soft_skills = ["leadership", "communication", "teamwork", "problem-solving",
"adaptability", "creativity", "time management", "empathy", "critical thinking"]

experience_keywords = ["managed", "developed", "designed", "created", "led",
"implemented", "analysed", "coordinated", "improved", "engineered"]
```

Three simple keyword lists that reflect modern resume expectations.

Step 2: Write the Analyser Function

Here's the core:

```python
def analyse_resume(text):
```

```
    text = text.lower()

    hard_score = 0

    soft_score = 0

    experience_score = 0


    for word in hard_skills:

        if word in text:

            hard_score += 1

    for word in soft_skills:

        if word in text:

            soft_score += 1

    for word in experience_keywords:

        if word in text:

            experience_score += 1


    return hard_score, soft_score, experience_score
```

Simple:

- Look for how many key elements are present.

- Give a quick evaluation.

Step 3: Build the Main App

Let's make it interactive:

```python
print(" Welcome to the Mini Resume Analyser!")

print("Paste your resume text below (or type 'exit' to quit).")


while True:

    resume_text = input("\nPaste your resume text: ")

    if resume_text.lower() == "exit":

        print(" Goodbye!")

        break


    hard, soft, experience = analyse_resume(resume_text)


    print("\n Resume Analysis:")

    print(f"- Hard skills mentioned: {hard}")

    print(f"- Soft skills mentioned: {soft}")

    print(f"- Experience action verbs: {experience}")


    total_score = hard + soft + experience
```

```
if total_score >= 15:

    print(" Strong resume! You're well-prepared.")

elif total_score >= 8:

    print(" Good resume, but could be improved by adding more skills and
examples.")

else:

    print(" Resume may be too weak. Add more skills, achievements, and
leadership verbs.")
```

Example in Action

User pastes:

"Developed web applications using Python and JavaScript. Led a team of engineers to build machine learning models. Skilled in communication and adaptability."

Output:

Resume Analysis:

- Hard skills mentioned: 4

- Soft skills mentioned: 2

- Experience action verbs: 2

Good resume, but could be improved by adding more skills and examples.

What Readers Learn from This Project

Skill	Practical Value
Text analysis	Practical AI-based scanning
Keyword scoring	Basic AI decision-making
Real-world app building	Useful for careers and freelancing
User-driven evaluation	Building feedback systems

Bonus Challenge Ideas (Optional Enhancements)

- **Add sections**: education, certifications, portfolio links.

- **Auto-highlight missing words**: "Consider mentioning 'teamwork' and 'SQL'."

- **Save analysis report**: Export to a text file.

- **Connect to a web form**: Build it into a mini resume web app later!

Conclusion

In less than 1 hour, readers:

- Built a **useful, real-world AI tool**

- Gained confidence analysing text data

- Made something **instantly helpful** for career growth or side hustles!

Chapter 9: Adding AI Magic to Web Apps: Smarter Chatbots, Image Analysis, and More Online

---

9.1 You've Built Apps... Now Make Them Smart and Public!

You've already:

- Built mini Python apps

- Built simple web apps

- Built basic AI tools

Now, imagine **putting all of it together**:

- Web apps **powered by AI**

- Online tools that **understand**, **analyse**, **interact** with users

- Apps you can **share with anyone on Earth**

This is where everything gets **excitingly real**.

9.2 The Game Plan

In this chapter, we'll: Build a **Web-Based Sentiment Analyser**

Build a **Web-Based AI Chatbot**

Discuss how to **prepare your app for real-world launch**

Show you the **basic structure of scalable AI apps**

You'll create apps that feel *alive* to users — all from simple, understandable Python code!

9.3 Setting Up: Flask + AI Libraries Review

You need:

- **Flask** for the web server.

- **Simple AI logic** (from your previous mini-projects).

- **Basic HTML forms** to collect user input.

If you don't have Flask yet:

pip install flask

Build 1: Web-Based Sentiment Analyser App

Step 1: Create the App Structure

Your project folder will look like:

sentiment_webapp/

├── app.py

└── templates/

    └── index.html

Step 2: app.py — Backend Python Code

from flask import Flask, request, render_template

```python
app = Flask(__name__)


positive_words = ["good", "happy", "great", "fantastic", "awesome", "amazing", "love",
"excellent", "nice", "joy"]

negative_words = ["bad", "sad", "terrible", "horrible", "worst", "awful", "hate", "angry",
"poor", "pain"]


def analyse_sentiment(text):

    text = text.lower()

    positive_score = sum(1 for word in positive_words if word in text)

    negative_score = sum(1 for word in negative_words if word in text)


    if positive_score > negative_score:

        return " Positive Sentiment"

    elif negative_score > positive_score:

        return " Negative Sentiment"

    else:

        return " Neutral Sentiment"
```

```python
@app.route("/", methods=["GET", "POST"])

def home():

    result = ""

    if request.method == "POST":

        user_text = request.form["user_text"]

        result = analyse_sentiment(user_text)

    return render_template("index.html", result=result)


if __name__ == "__main__":

    app.run(debug=True)
```

Step 3: templates/index.html — Frontend Page

```html
<!DOCTYPE html>

<html>

<head>

    <title>AI Sentiment Analyser</title>

</head>

<body>

    <h1> AI Sentiment Analyser</h1>

    <form method="POST">
```

```html
<textarea name="user_text" rows="6" cols="50" placeholder="Paste your text here..."></textarea><br><br>

    <button type="submit">Analyse</button>

  </form>


  {% if result %}

  <h2>Result: {{ result }}</h2>

  {% endif %}

</body>

</html>
```

Now when you run:

python app.py

Visit http://127.0.0.1:5000/ and boom!

You have a **live, AI-powered website** that analyses text sentiment!

Build 2: Web-Based AI Chatbot App

Step 1: Create Chatbot Project Folder

chatbot_webapp/

├── app.py

└── templates/

    └── index.html

Step 2: app.py — Backend Python Code

```python
from flask import Flask, request, render_template


app = Flask(__name__)


def simple_chatbot(message):

    message = message.lower()

    if "hello" in message:

        return "Hi there! "

    elif "how are you" in message:

        return "I'm doing great, thanks for asking! "

    elif "bye" in message:

        return "Goodbye! "

    else:

        return "Hmm... I didn't understand that. "
```

```python
@app.route("/", methods=["GET", "POST"])

def home():

    response = ""

    if request.method == "POST":

        user_message = request.form["user_message"]

        response = simple_chatbot(user_message)

    return render_template("index.html", response=response)


if __name__ == "__main__":

    app.run(debug=True)
```

Step 3: templates/index.html

```html
<!DOCTYPE html>

<html>

<head>

    <title>Simple AI Chatbot</title>

</head>

<body>

    <h1>☐ Talk to Our Chatbot</h1>

    <form method="POST">
```

```
    <input type="text" name="user_message" placeholder="Say something..."
size="50"><br><br>

    <button type="submit">Send</button>

  </form>


  {% if response %}

  <h2>Bot says: {{ response }}</h2>

  {% endif %}

</body>

</html>
```

Now run:

python app.py

Chat with your own **live AI chatbot** running locally on your machine!

What's Really Happening

Part	What It Does
Flask app	Handles the communication between user and server
HTML form	Collects user input

Part	What It Does
AI function	Analyses input and returns a smart response
Result display	Shows the AI's output instantly

You've created a **live online smart app** — with less than 100 lines of code!

What Readers Learn in This Chapter

Skill	Practical Value
Flask routes	Handle user actions on a website
HTML forms + Python logic	Real interactivity
AI + Web	Combine intelligence with accessibility
App structure	How professional small apps are built

Conclusion

In **this chapter**, you:

- Built **AI-powered websites**

- Understood **how to handle real user input**

- Published **dynamic, smart web apps**

- Took the first step toward **professional online apps**

You're not just coding anymore —

You're building the future.

9.9 What's Next?

Now that you know how to put AI on websites...

You'll learn **how to prepare your web apps for the real Internet**:

- Host them online

- Let anyone access them

- Start building a **portfolio** of your work

Next chapter: How to Launch Your AI-Powered Web Apps Online!

We'll use beginner-friendly tools to **put your creations on the Internet** for real

users!

(End of Chapter 9)

Progress Update

Chapter	Status
Introduction	Complete
Chapters 1–8	Complete
Chapter 9	Complete

1-Hour Project: "AI Name Generator Web App — Create Unique Names with Python"

Project Overview

We'll build a **tiny web app** where:

- Users can generate **cool, unique names** for businesses, projects, characters, apps, etc.

- Python will **combine random words** to create fresh name ideas.

Teaches random generation, simple web form handling, creativity boosting apps — very popular for portfolios!

Step-by-Step Plan

Step 1: Create Your Project Structure

name_generator_webapp/

├── app.py

```
└── templates/

    └── index.html
```

This keeps it clean and organized.

Step 2: app.py — Backend Python Code

```python
from flask import Flask, render_template, request

import random


app = Flask(__name__)


adjectives = ["Brave", "Happy", "Clever", "Bright", "Swift", "Silent", "Fierce", "Mighty",
"Bold", "Lucky"]

nouns = ["Lion", "River", "Sky", "Forest", "Mountain", "Star", "Knight", "Dream",
"Phoenix", "Voyager"]


def generate_name():

    return random.choice(adjectives) + " " + random.choice(nouns)


@app.route("/", methods=["GET", "POST"])

def home():
```

```
new_name = ""

if request.method == "POST":

    new_name = generate_name()

return render_template("index.html", name=new_name)


if __name__ == "__main__":

    app.run(debug=True)
```

- Randomly **combines one adjective + one noun** to create a name.

- Refreshes a new name **each time** the user clicks.

Step 3: templates/index.html — Frontend Web Page

```html
<!DOCTYPE html>

<html>

<head>

    <title>AI Name Generator</title>

</head>

<body>

    <h1> AI Name Generator</h1>

    <form method="POST">
```

```
<button type="submit">Generate New Name</button>
```

```
</form>
```

```
{% if name %}
```

```
<h2>Your Generated Name: {{ name }}</h2>
```

```
{% endif %}
```

```
</body>
```

```
</html>
```

- One simple button.

- Every click brings up a fresh new name suggestion!

Example in Action

User clicks "Generate New Name" → App displays:

Your Generated Name: Swift Knight

Click again → Another one:

Your Generated Name: Lucky Voyager

Fun, fast, creative!

What Readers Learn from This Project

Skill	Practical Value
Random choice generation	Power behind games, content, creative tools
Web form handling	Real user-triggered actions
Dynamic page update	Real-world web interactivity
Creative app development	Useful for portfolios and fun personal projects

---

Bonus Challenge Ideas (Optional Enhancements)

- **Let users pick themes:** Fantasy, Tech, Business.

- **Allow multiple name generation at once:** List 5–10 options.

- **Save favorite names:** Build a simple "save to list" function.

- **Offer .com domain checks:** Connect to domain availability APIs.

Conclusion

In **less than 1 hour**, the reader:

- Built another **AI-enhanced interactive web app**

- Practiced creative programming with random generation

- Created a project they can **demo in a portfolio** or **use for fun!**

Now You're Ready:

You've built enough to **launch apps live on the Internet** next!

Time for **Chapter 10**:

"Launching Your AI Apps Online: A Beginner's Guide to Hosting"

Where we'll show how to **deploy** your apps and make them **publicly accessible worldwide**!

Chapter 10: Launching Your AI Apps Online — A Beginner's Guide to Hosting

---

10.1 Why Hosting Changes Everything

So far:

- You built cool apps

- You built smart AI features

- You even built web interfaces

But they're all **only on your computer**.

Hosting =

Making your apps **available to anyone on the Internet**.

It's the difference between:

- *Private project → Public impact*

- *Local app → Global service*

- *Learning → Entrepreneurship*

You're about to **level up** big time!

10.2 What You'll Learn

The easiest ways to host your apps

Step-by-step to put your Flask app online

Basic free hosting using **Render** (best for beginners)

What comes after: scaling up, upgrading, professional hosting

You'll **actually deploy your app today** — not just theory!

10.3 Hosting Options (Beginner-Friendly)

Option	Best For	Difficulty	Free?
Render	Web apps like yours	Very Easy	Free tier
Vercel (with Flask adapter)	Static sites & simple Python	Medium	Free
Heroku (Python apps)	Python servers, APIs	Medium (needs Git)	Free (basic)
Professional Cloud (AWS, Azure, GCP)	Huge apps, companies	Hard	Paid

We'll use **Render** — the easiest, fastest for your current level.

10.4 Step-by-Step: Deploying to Render.com

Step 1: Prepare Your App

You need these files in your app folder:

- app.py (your main code)

- requirements.txt (list of libraries your app needs)

- templates/ folder with your .html files

Create requirements.txt easily:

- Open your terminal where your app is.

- Type:

pip freeze > requirements.txt

This command grabs all installed libraries and writes them into requirements.txt.

Step 2: Create a GitHub Repository

Render pulls your app from GitHub.

If you don't have GitHub yet:

- Go to github.com

- Create a free account

Then:

- Create a new repository (click "New Repo")

- Name it something simple like my-ai-app

- **Do NOT** initialize with a README (empty repo)

Now upload (push) your app folder to GitHub.

If you're new to Git:

- Install Git: https://git-scm.com/

- In your app folder terminal:

git init

git add .

git commit -m "First commit"

git branch -M main

git remote add origin https://github.com/yourusername/your-repo-name.git

git push -u origin main

Your app is now on GitHub!

Step 3: Set Up Your App on Render

1. Go to https://render.com/

2. Create a free account

3. Click **"New Web Service"**

4. Connect to your GitHub account

5. Choose your app's repository

6. Fill in:

   - **Name:** anything you like

   - **Environment:** Python

   - **Build Command:**

- o pip install -r requirements.txt

- o **Start Command:**

- o gunicorn app:app

You might need to install gunicorn locally too:

pip install gunicorn

And add it to requirements.txt (add gunicorn manually if not auto-added).

Step 4: Deploy!

- Click **Create Web Service**

- Wait a minute or two for it to build and deploy

- Render will give you a **live link** like:

https://your-app-name.onrender.com

Visit it — **your app is live!**

You can send this link to anyone in the world!

10.5 Troubleshooting Tips

Problem   **Quick Solution**

App crashes instantly Check if your Python file is named app.py

Missing library error   Make sure requirements.txt includes everything

Problem	Quick Solution
404 or no route found	Check your @app.route("/") setup
Gunicorn error	Double-check gunicorn app:app command syntax

Most small issues are **easy to fix** with clear error messages!

10.6 Quick Recap: You Just Launched a Public AI App!

What You Learned	Why It Matters
Create requirements.txt	Tell servers what libraries you use
Upload to GitHub	Share your code online
Use Render	Deploy free, real, public apps
Make apps accessible	Anyone can now use your creations!

You're no longer just a Python coder —

You are now a **public app creator**.

Conclusion

You:

- Built smart apps

- Built web interfaces

- Hosted real apps online

You've **completed the full beginner-to-creator cycle**.

This is the foundation that launches **freelancers, entrepreneurs, and future AI innovators**!

10.7 What's Next?

From here, the possibilities explode:

- Build **better web designs** (CSS, Bootstrap)

- Add **databases** (save user data)

- Train **custom AI models**

- Create **mobile apps connected to your AI**

- Monetize your apps (offer them as services!)

You're now ready to **build, launch, and scale** anything you imagine.

(End of Chapter 10)

Progress Update

Chapter	Status
Introduction	Complete
Chapters 1–9	Complete

Chapter	Status
Chapter 10	Complete

Bonus Chapter 1: From Apps to Business — Turning Your Projects Into Income

B1.1 Welcome to the Creator Economy

You're not just building apps for fun anymore.

You now have the **skills to create tools that solve problems,** help people — and **make money**.

The truth today is simple:

If you can build useful tools, you can build your own career.

You don't need to beg for a job.

You **create your own opportunities**.

In this chapter, you'll learn **how to turn your AI-powered apps into income streams**.

B1.2 Main Income Paths for AI-Powered Python Creators

Path	Example	Potential
Freelancing	Build custom automations, chatbots, web apps	$30–$150/hour
Productizing Apps	Sell access to tools (SaaS)	$10–$50/month/user
Teaching	Courses, books, workshops	Unlimited
Consulting	Help businesses automate	$500–$5,000/project

Path	Example	Potential
Startups	Launch your own tech services	Unlimited (high risk, high reward)

B1.3 Step 1: Pick a Problem Your App Solves

Every profitable app **solves a problem**.

Examples:

- Sentiment Analyser → Help brands monitor reviews automatically.

- Resume Analyser → Help job seekers optimize resumes.

- Name Generator → Help startups, marketers create brand names.

- File Organizer → Help small businesses tidy up digital chaos.

Tip:

If someone would pay to save time, get better results, or feel smarter — it's a good app idea.

B1.4 Step 2: Package Your App for Real Users

Real users need:

- A **simple** website (no complex installation)

- **Clear benefits** ("Save 5 hours/week!")

- **Easy access** (one-click signup or payment)

You can:

- **Host on Render** (free for early users)

- **Add a simple pricing page** later

- **Collect emails** if you want to grow a user base

B1.5 Step 3: Start with Free + Paid Options

Smart strategy:

- Let people use a **basic free version**.

- Offer a **Pro version** with extras (more features, faster analysis, saved history, etc.)

This is called **Freemium** —

and it's the model behind giants like Dropbox, Canva, and Spotify!

B1.6 Step 4: Find Your First Users

Start simple:

- Share your app on LinkedIn, Reddit, X (formerly Twitter), Product Hunt.

- Post helpful demos showing how it works.

- Ask early users for feedback ("What's missing? What's great?")

Bonus:

Early users often become your **best marketers**!

B1.7 Step 5: Charge When You're Ready

Once your app solves a real pain point consistently:

- Offer monthly subscriptions ($5–$20/month)

- Offer one-time payments ($20–$100/app)

- Offer consulting services around it ($200–$1000+ per project)

You don't have to be perfect.

You just have to be useful.

Conclusion of Bonus 1

You already have:

- Working apps

- Skills to improve them

- Ability to share them online

Now you have the knowledge to: Start freelancing

Launch micro-products

Build income streams from your Python journey

You're not just a coder.

You're a **creator**.

(End of Bonus Chapter 1)

Bonus Chapter 2: Advanced AI Tricks — Smarter Models Without Heavy Coding

B2.1 Welcome to the Next Level of AI Creation

AI might sound intimidating:

Neural networks, transformers, embeddings...

Good news:

Today you can use powerful AI models without building them from scratch.

Thanks to pre-built tools and APIs,

you can create **smarter, more powerful apps** almost instantly.

In this chapter, you'll learn **how to supercharge your apps with powerful AI services —**

without needing heavy machine learning knowledge.

B2.2 Powerful AI Services You Can Easily Integrate

Service	What It Does	Example Usage
OpenAI API (ChatGPT, GPT-4)	Smart text understanding, content generation	Smart assistants, blog writers
Hugging Face Inference API	Text, image, audio AI models	Sentiment analysis, text summarizers
DeepAI API	Image recognition, face detection, colorization	Build visual tools
AssemblyAI API	Speech-to-text, audio intelligence	Build voice note analysers

All have **simple Python wrappers** and **free tiers** to start.

B2.3 Example: Connect Your Web App to ChatGPT API

Imagine **your own AI assistant** inside your web app!

Step 1: Install OpenAI Python Library

pip install openai

Step 2: Set Up OpenAI API Key

- Create an account at https://platform.openai.com/

- Get your free API key.

In your app:

import openai

openai.api_key = "your-api-key-here"

Step 3: Write a Function to Talk to GPT

def ask_gpt(prompt):

  response = openai.ChatCompletion.create(

    model="gpt-3.5-turbo",

    messages=[{"role": "user", "content": prompt}]

```
)

    return response['choices'][0]['message']['content']
```

Now you can **send any user message** and get **a smart AI reply**!

B2.4 Example: Plug GPT into Your Flask Chatbot App

Update your chatbot like this:

```
@app.route("/", methods=["GET", "POST"])

def home():

    bot_response = ""

    if request.method == "POST":

        user_message = request.form["user_message"]

        bot_response = ask_gpt(user_message)

    return render_template("index.html", response=bot_response)
```

Congratulations —

you just **created your own GPT-powered web app**!

B2.5 Other Advanced AI Features You Can Add Easily

Feature	How to Add
Sentiment Analysis	Hugging Face's sentiment model
Image Captioning	DeepAI's image caption generator
Audio Transcription	AssemblyAI speech-to-text

Almost all of them are as simple as:

- Install a library

- Get an API key

- Send a request and receive the AI response

No need to build neural networks from scratch!

Conclusion of Bonus 2

You now know how to:

- Build smarter apps

- Add text understanding, vision, voice AI easily

- Use the most powerful AI tools available today

You are not limited anymore.

You can build tools that: Think better

Help more people

Grow bigger businesses

This is just the beginning.

The world of AI is **yours to build.**

(End of Bonus Chapter 2)

Progress Update

Section	Status
Introduction	Complete
Chapters 1–10	Complete
Bonus Chapter 1 (Business)	Complete
Bonus Chapter 2 (Advanced AI)	Complete

Epilogue: Your Journey Is Just Beginning

When you started this book, maybe you doubted yourself a little.

"Can I really learn Python?"

"Can I actually build real apps?"

"Is AI too complicated for me?"

And yet — here you are.

You wrote real Python code.

You built apps that automate, create, predict, and serve.

You launched AI-powered web apps live to the world.

You learned how to turn your creations into income and opportunity.

You didn't just **read** this book.

You built yourself up into a creator.

That's the real power.

You Are No Longer Just a Consumer of Technology

Most people today use apps, websites, and AI tools built by others.

You?

You now **build the future**.

You've crossed a line that 99% of people will never cross.

From user → to creator.

From consumer → to innovator.

This is rare.

This is powerful.

This is just the beginning.

Where You Go From Here

You now have everything you need to:

- Start a freelance career

- Launch your own micro-startup

- Create passive income tools

- Build a portfolio to impress any employer

- Solve real-world problems with technology

- Bring your boldest ideas to life

You're armed with skills, tools, and — most importantly — the **mindset** of a builder.

Nothing stops a determined builder.

Not today. Not ever.

A Final Secret

Here's the real secret successful creators know:

The first 10 projects you build will be clunky, simple, and sometimes ugly.

The next 10 projects will be better.

The next 50 projects will be amazing.

And one day, something you build will change someone's life — maybe even your own.

You don't need to be perfect.

You just need to **keep building**.

Each small app you launch...

Each idea you test...

Each challenge you face and figure out...

Every single one is a stepping stone to mastery, freedom, and impact.

Final Words

So here's your mission, if you choose to accept it:

Build small projects — often and fearlessly.

Launch them publicly — even if they're not perfect.

Help people — even if it's one user at a time.

Keep learning — Python, AI, automation, business.

Never stop creating.

You're no longer just following technology.

You're **leading it**.

The future belongs to builders like you.

Now —

go make it real.

(End of Epilogue)

Full Completion Update:

Section	Status
Introduction	Complete
Chapters 1–10	Complete

Section	Status
Bonus Chapter 1	Complete
Bonus Chapter 2	Complete
Epilogue	Complete

About the Author

Education:

- Doctor of Science (DSc) in Project Evaluation, Technion, Haifa, Israel

- Master of Science (MSc) in Operations Research, London School of Economics

- Bachelor of Science (BSc) in Industrial and Management Engineering, Technion, Haifa, Israel

Teaching and Academic Research Positions Held:

- Micro Economics

- Macro Economics

- Econometrics

- Statistics

- Mathematics

- Public Finance

- Urban Planning Mathematical Models

- Transportation Science

Urban and Regional Planning Experience:

- Comprehensive Urban Renewal Project Manager (Physical and Social Project) of the East Acco Government Project. Received the title Yakir Acco from the Acco municipality.

Mathematical Modelling Projects:

- Optimal production mix model using linear programming for the Israeli Paper Mill, Hedera.

- Optimal loading and unloading of ships in Ashdod port using mathematical simulation and integer programming models for the Phosphates at the Negev company.

- Optimal mining order for the Phosphates at the Negev company using mathematical linear, integer, and nonlinear programming.

- Optimal ship operation to transport crude oil using a simulation model for the Institute of By Sea Transport at Haifa.

- Traffic assignment mathematical model for the Transportation Science Institute, Technion, Haifa.

- Industrial Land use analysis in the city of Tel Aviv using Principal Factors Analysis for Tel Aviv Municipality.

- Pupils distribution among the Tel Aviv school system using an integer programming model for the Municipality of Tel Aviv.

- Various mathematical programming models for El Al, The Electric Company, Teva, etc., in association with the Representative of SAS in Israel (Maia Computers).

- Truck fleet routing model based on mathematical programming and heuristics models for international clientele.

- Optimal Locomotive and personnel assignment (run cutting problem) to trains using integer programming models for the New York City Transit Authority.

- Statistical analysis for sales for the American Cyanamid company in Pearl River, New Jersey.

- Sales analysis models (econometric and statistical models) for JC Penny, USA.

Professional Experience:

- Founding partner (2006-2011) in the company "Kaul and Lomovasky Holdings Inc" specializing in the computerization of trading using artificial intelligence.

- Internet and Artificial Intelligence Programmer, Developer, and Consultant (2012-2018).

- Developed an AI-based system to calculate the price of apartments in 300 towns in Israel, using VBA Excel Neural Networks (artificial intelligence) pre-processing and presented the prices on a Python Django-based website.

- Author of several books on topics such as Futurology, Python, algorithmic trading, quantum computing, crypto trading, artificial intelligence, Urbanism, Economics, Public Policy, Operations Research, Tariffs and Trade Wars and startup ideas.

Computer Programming Skills:

- C, VBA under Excel, Microsoft Office, HTML, PHP, MATLAB, SAS, Python, Django, Keras, Panda, Cloud AI Applications, TensorFlow, Google Cloud Platform, OpenCV, Adversarial GANs, Computer Vision, Image Classification, Object Recognition, Pose Recognition.

- Quantum computing and quantum machine learning.

Algorithm development, end-to-end ownership.

Related Publications (2018-2025)

-Algorithmic Trading with Python Amid Tariffs and Trade Wars: Foundations to AI Strategies (The 2025–2030 Manual): Beginners Friendly. Python Code Explained ... Discussed Thoroughly (Economic Turbulence) Kindle Edition

by Dr Israel Carlos Lomovasky (Author) Format: Kindle Edition

-Tariffs, Trade Wars and the Magnificent Seven Stocks: Trading and Investing 2025–2030: Apple, Microsoft, Alphabet, Amazon, Meta, Nvidia and Tesla. (Economic Turbulence) Kindle Edition

by Dr Israel Carlos Lomovasky (Author) Format: Kindle Edition

-Navigating Trade Wars and Technological Shifts: 12 Startup Opportunities (2025–2027): Turning Tariff Tensions into Breakthrough Startup Models Based on Cutting Edge High Tech (Economic Turbulence) Kindle Edition

by Dr Israel Carlos Lomovasky (Author) Format: Kindle Edition

-US–China Trade War: Current Status, Scenarios, and Investment Strategy (2025 – 2026): Turn the turbulence of geopolitical tension into your next investment advantage Kindle Edition

by Dr Israel Carlos Lomovasky (Author) Format: Kindle Edition

-Day Trading Equities, ETFs, Options, Futures , Amid Global Trade Wars and Tariffs (2025 Report): Beginners to Advanced. Real Time Strategies and Examples. Global and US Markets (Economic Turbulence) Kindle Edition

by Dr Israel Carlos Lomovasky (Author) Format: Kindle Edition

-Safeguard and Prosper: Mastering Portfolio Strategy Amid Tariffs and Trade Wars. Portfolio Protecting Briefing 2025: Is your Investment Portfolio Ready ... and Tariff Turbulence (Economic Turbulence) Kindle Edition

by Dr Israel Carlos Lomovasky (Author) Format: Kindle Edition

-Making Money Under Tariffs and Trade Wars. Business Ideas Briefing: Strategies like Import Substitution, Reshoring Partnerships, Tariff Arbitrage, and Specialized Consulting (Economic Turbulence) Kindle Edition

by Dr Israel Carlos Lomovasky (Author) Format: Kindle Edition

-Tariffs and the Stock Market: Trading and Investing in a Turbulent Economy: The Knowledge you (Seasoned or Beginner) Need, to Trade and Invest Profitably in These Tumultuous Times. Kindle Edition

by Dr Israel Carlos Lomovasky (Author) Format: Kindle Edition

- Navigating the Storm: A Comprehensive Guide to Thriving Amid Trade Wars and Tariff Uncertainty: Practical Strategies for Citizens, Businesses, Governments ... and Prosper Globally (Economic Turbulence) Kindle Edition

by Dr Israel Carlos Lomovasky (Author) Format: Kindle Edition

-One World, One Future: Overcoming National Divisions Through Global Governance and Decentralized Democracy: A Visionary Blueprint :a Planet-Wide Government ... Minds Social Direct Democracy (MOTMSDD)) Kindle Edition

by Dr Israel Carlos Lomovasky (Author) Format: Kindle Edition

-AI for Business: Strategies for Non-Technical Managers: Comprehensive yet Digestible, Practical Advice, Real-World Success Stories, Future insights- a ... learning-Python Book 5) Kindle Edition

by Dr Israel Carlos Lomovasky (Author) Format: Kindle Edition

-The Journey to Humanity's Far Future : Crucial Questions that Need to be Explored Pushing the Edge of Imagination: State of the Art Ongoing Futurology ... - Futurology - Futurism - Science Fiction) Kindle Edition

by Dr Israel Carlos Lomovasky (Author) Format: Kindle Edition

-Future Foundations: A Beginner's Guide to Futurology for Business, Government, and Beyond: Your Complete Roadmap to Exploring and Shaping Tomorrow's World! (Futures sciences - Futurology - Futurism) Kindle Edition

by Dr Israel Carlos Lomovasky (Author) Format: Kindle Edition

-The Future of Conflict Resolution: Harnessing Technology and Human-Centered Approaches: AI, Hybrid AI-Human, Blockchain, BCI, Neuroscience, Virtual Reality, MOTMSDD, Quantum, Restorative Justice Kindle Edition

by Dr Israel Carlos Lomovasky (Author) Format: Kindle Edition

-AutoML Meets Real Estate: A No-Code Approach to Property Tech Innovation: Comprehensive ,Beginner-Friendly, with Step-by-Step Guidance for Real-World PropTech Projects. Kindle Edition

by Dr Israel Carlos lomovasky (Author) Format: Kindle Edition

-The AutoML Edge: Creating High-Performance Trading Algorithms Without Coding: AutoML Democratizes Algorithmic Trading, Enabling Traders to Leverage the Power of Machine Learning without Writing Code Kindle Edition

by Dr Israel Carlos Lomovasky (Author) Format: Kindle Edition

-AI Made Simple: How AutoML is Changing Business Without Coding: No Code, Low Code, Practical, Beginners to Advanced, Marketing, Finance, Healthcare, Retail, ... learning-Python Book 4) Kindle Edition

by Dr Israel Carlos Lomovasky (Author) Format: Kindle Edition

-Minds, Machines, and the Metropolis: How MOTMSDD, AI, and IoT Will Reimagine Urban Life: Future of Urbanism with Metaverse of the Minds Social Direct Democracy ... & Cutting Edge, Sustainable Technologies Kindle Edition

by Dr Israel Carlos Lomovasky (Author) Format: Kindle Edition

-The Profitable Algorithmic Trading Manual with AI/ML and Python for Beginners to Advanced: Retail & Institutional. Stocks, ETFs, Forex, Crypto, Options, More. Developing, Deploying & Scaling Kindle Edition

by Dr Israel Carlos Lomovasky (Author) Format: Kindle Edition

-PropTech Innovation with Python: A Complete Step-by-Step Guide with Applied Real Estate Code Examples: Real Estate Revolution: Encyclopedic PropTech Solutions with Python, Foundations to Advanced Kindle Edition

by Dr Israel Carlos Lomovasky (Author) Format: Kindle Edition

-PropTech (Property Technology): Analysing the Impact of Technology on Real Estate Finance.: Blockchain, Smart Contracts, AI/ML in Property Management. Smart Buildings & Virtual and Augmented Reality Kindle Edition

by Dr Israel Carlos lomovasky (Author) Format: Kindle Edition

-Democracy Reimagined: Exposing Populism and Charting a Path to a True Democratic Revival: Populism Unveiled: Democratic Innovations for a Resilient Future ... Minds Social Direct Democracy (MOTMSDD)) Kindle Edition

by Dr Israel Carlos Lomovasky (Author) Format: Kindle Edition

-Crypto Market Mechanics: A New Playbook for Investors and Traders: Crypto Specific: Economics, Correlations, Global Events, Psychology, Risk, Diversification, ... AI Algos, Technical Analysis & Indicators Kindle Edition

by Dr Israel Carlos Lomovasky (Author) Format: Kindle Edition

-Crypto for Beginners: A Step-by-Step Guide to Digital Currency Investing and Trading: Comprehensive and Detailed Guide to Cryptocurrency Investing, Including ... the Blockchain Industry (FINANCE Book 11) Kindle Edition

by Dr Israel Carlos Lomovasky (Author) Format: Kindle Edition

Book 8 of 8: FINANCE

-Quantum Wealth: Mastering Investments in the Quantum Computing Boom.: Quantum Opportunities: Investing in Breakthrough Technologies. Foundations to Advanced. Kindle Edition

by Dr Israel Carlos Lomovasky (Author) Format: Kindle Edition

-AI Investment Mastery: How to Outperform the Market with AI Assets: Comprehensive. Investing in AI Stocks, ETFs, Mutual Funds, Venture Capital, Private ... Foundations to Advanced (FINANCE Book 9) Kindle Edition

by Dr Israel Carlos Lomovasky (Author) Format: Kindle Edition

Book 8 of 8: FINANCE

-The Quantum Nexus: AI, Blockchain, and the Future of Everything: How these Cutting-edge Technologies will Converge to Reshape Various Industries and Everyday ... - Futurology - Science fiction Book 8) Kindle Edition

by Dr Israel Carlos Lomovasky (Author) Format: Kindle Edition

Book 7 of 7: Future sciences - Futurology - Science fiction

-Coding the Citizen's Voice: Python Tools for MOTMSDD in Governance and Planning: the Manual: Python Source Code. AI & Data Science. Metaverse of the Minds ... and Brain Computer Interface Book 9) Kindle Edition

by Dr Israel Carlos Lomovasky (Author) Format: Kindle Edition

Book 8 of 8: The future implications of the combination between the Internet, the Metaverse and Brain Computer Interface

-Beyond the Vote: AI Applications in Direct Democracy and Civic Engagement: Integrating AI, ML, NLP, Data Visualization, and MOTMSDD Into Public Governance ... and Brain Computer Interface Book 8) Kindle Edition

by Dr Israel Carlos Lomovasky (Author) Format: Kindle Edition

Beyond Quantum: The Next Leap in Computational Paradigms: Exploring the Future of Advanced Computing Technologies (Quantum Computing Book 5) Kindle Edition

by Dr Israel Carlos Lomovasky (Author) Format: Kindle Edition

Book 5 of 5: Quantum Computing

-AI-Proof Your Career: Building Resilience in the Face of Automation: Strategies for Healthcare,Finance,Manufacturing,Art,Entertainment,Retail, Transportation,Energy,Logistics,Government,Teaching Kindle Edition

by Dr Israel Carlos Lomovasky (Author) Format: **Kindle Edition**

-Defensive Trading in Crypto ETFs: Protecting Your Portfolio in Volatile Markets: The Damage and Losses Control Bible for The Crypto ETFs Investor and Trader Kindle Edition

by Dr Israel Carlos Lomovasky (Author) Format: **Kindle Edition**

Book 11 of 11: TRADING

-Algorithmic Trading for Everyone: A Non-Programmer's Journey to Automation: Comprehensive Introduction to Algo Trading for Beginners Without Programming Background Kindle Edition

by Dr Israel Carlos Lomovasky (Author) Format: **Kindle Edition**

Book 10 of 10: TRADING

-The Great Crypto Illusion: Navigating the Future of Valueless Assets : Examining the Sustainability of Cryptocurrencies Without Traditional Intrinsic Value. (FINANCE Book 8) Kindle Edition

by Dr Israel Carlos Lomovasky (Author) Format: **Kindle Edition**

-Navigating Crypto ETFs Trading: An Absolute Beginners Guide to New Markets: Foundations of Crypto ETF Trading: Building Your Digital Investment Portfolio Kindle Edition

by Dr Israel Carlos Lomovasky (Author) Format: **Kindle Edition**

-Profit and Protect: Retail Trading Strategies to Manage Risk and Grow Your Wealth: Foundations to Advanced. Stocks, Bonds, Crypto, Commodities & Forex. Hedging with Options, Swaps, Futures & More Kindle Edition

by Dr Israel Carlos Lomovasky (Author) Format: Kindle Edition

-The Future Game: Unleashing AI and Quantum Computing Power in Game Theory.: Beginners to Advanced.Python Code.Case studies:Economics,Finance,Politics,Environment,Social Science,Psychology,Health,More Kindle Edition

By Dr Israel Carlos Lomovasky (Author) Format: Kindle Edition

-AI and Quantum Strategies: Python's Role in Economic Innovation: Foundations to Advanced. With python and Quantum Code in a Computational Economics Range of Case Studies Kindle Edition

by Dr Israel Carlos Lomovasky (Author) Format: Kindle Edition

-Quantum Computing in Finance: Bridging Theory and Practice with Python: Case Studies: Algorithmic Trading, Risk Management, Fraud Detection, Options Pricing ,Economic Forecasting and more

by Dr Israel Carlos Lomovasky (Author)

Book 6 of 6: FINANCE

-Artificial Gods: The Onset of Superior Machine Intelligence and Consciousness: : The Why and How of a Ban on Research Leading To Superintelligence And AI Consciousness Kindle Edition

by Dr Israel Carlos Lomovasky (Author)

-Quantum and Consciousness: Exploring the Mind-Computer Interface: Unveiling the Quantum Mind: Quantum Computing and the Fabric of Consciousness Kindle Edition
by Dr Israel Carlos Lomovasky (Author)

-Quantum Democracy: Unleashing MOTMSDD with Quantum Computing: MOTMSDD : Metaverse Of The Minds Social Direct Democracy (The future implications of the ... and Brain Computer Interface Book 6) Kindle Edition
by Dr Israel Carlos Lomovasky (Author)

-MOTMSDD: Metaverse Of The Minds Social Direct Democracy: Governance and Public Decision Making in The Era of Brain Computer Interface, AI and Metaverse, ... and Brain Computer Interface Book 5) Kindle Edition
by Dr Israel Carlos Lomovasky (Author)

-MOTMSDD Urbanism:Redefining Cities through AI and Metaverse of the Minds Social Direct Democracy: Sustainable Urbanism in the Age of Brain-Computer Interface.Solving Conflicts between Citizen's Needs Kindle Edition
by Dr Israel Carlos Lomovasky (Author)

-AI in Financial Markets: A Guide to Algorithmic Trading with ChatGPT: Python Code. CHATGPT Assistance. Basics to Advanced. Traditional and AI/ML Trading. (FINANCE Book 6) Kindle Edition
by Dr Israel Carlos Lomovasky (Author)

-Python for Financial Freedom: Algorithmic Strategies for Personal Wealth: Trading and Investing. Foundations to Advanced. AI/ML, Risk ,Tax ,and Money Management. Stocks & Crypto (FINANCE Book 5) Kindle Edition

by Dr Israel Carlos Lomovasky (Author)

-Quantum Foundations of Computer Vision: A Guide for Researchers and Practitioners: Python and Quantum Language Code. Future Proof Computer Vision (Quantum Computing Book 3) Kindle Edition

by Dr Israel Carlos Lomovasky (Author)

-MOTMSDD ECONOMICS: From Classical Economics, to Metaverse Of The Minds Social Direct Democracy Economics.: For The Next WELFARE ECONOMICS: Harnessing BCI ... the Metaverse . (FUTURE ECONOMICS Book 1) Kindle Edition

by Dr Israel Carlos Lomovasky (Author)

-Quantum Hedge: Unlocking the Future of Algorithmic Trading. : Python and Quantum Languages Code. Basics to Advanced. Stocks, Forex and Crypto. Theory and Hands on Practice. Kindle Edition

by Dr Israel Carlos Lomovasky (Author)

-Quantum Economics: Rethinking Macro and Micro in the Age of Quantum Computing: Theory and Practice: Python and Quantum Language Code Explained Step by Step (FUTURE ECONOMICS Book 2) Kindle Edition

by Dr Israel Carlos Lomovasky (Author)

-Driving with the Mind: Exploring MOTMSDD and Its Impact on Smart Cities and Autonomous Mobility: MOTMSDD: Metaverse of The Minds Social Direct Democracy: ... Meets The Metaverse (URBANISM Book 4) Kindle Edition

by Dr Israel Carlos Lomovasky (Author)

-AI in Fundamental Analysis: Uncovering Hidden Algorithmic Investment Opportunities with Python.: Machine,Reinforcement and Deep Learning.Complete AI-Driven ... Advanced.Risk Management. (FINANCE Book 2) Kindle Edition

by Dr Israel Carlos Lomovasky (Author)

-Python for AI and Creativity: Unleashing the Power of Artificial Intelligence in the Arts: Basics to Advanced.Visual Arts,Design,Music,Poetry,Storytelling, ... learning-Python Book 3) Kindle Edition

by Dr Israel Carlos Lomovasky (Author)

-Python for Machine Learning. From Intermediate to Advanced Guide With Code.: Unleash the Potential of Advanced Machine Learning in Python. Covering Many ... learning-Python Book 2) Kindle Edition

by Dr Israel Carlos Lomovasky (Author)

-Python for Smart Cities: Machine Learning and Artificial Intelligence Applications for Urban Planning and Infrastructure: Python in Action: ML/AI for Smart ... Infrastructure Management (URBANISM Book 2) Kindle Edition

by Dr Israel Carlos Lomovasky (Author)

-Python for Machine Learning: A Beginner's Guide.From Scratch to intermediate.: Basis For Algorithmic Finance, Trading, Healthcare, Industry, Transportation, ... learning-Python Book 1) Kindle Edition

by Dr Israel Carlos Lomovasky (Author)

-SINGULARITY'S VEIL: THE RISE AND FALL OF HUMANITY. : A TALE BETWEEN SCIENCE FICTION AND FUTUROLOGY. STOP ARTIFICIAL GENERAL INTELLIGENCE NOW. (Future sciences - Futurology - Science fiction Book 6) Kindle Edition

by Dr Israel Carlos Lomovasky (Author)

-KILLING THE BEAST. THE THREAT OF ADVANCING ARTIFICIAL GENERAL INTELLIGENCE.: A CALL TO BAN AGI.SURVIVAL OF HUMANITY ON THE LINE. A CONTRARIAN NARRATIVE ... - Futurology - Science fiction Book 5) Kindle Edition

by Dr Israel Carlos Lomovasky (Author)

-Day Trading Basics to Advanced:A Comprehensive Guide.From Scalping to AI/ML.Algorithmic Trading.Python Code.: Day Trading Decoded:Unlocking Secrets to Profitable Trading.Stocks,Crypto,Options,Forex Kindle Edition

by Dr Israel Carlos Lomovasky (Author)

-BEGINNER'S MACHINE LEARNING AND ARTIFICIAL INTELLIGENCE IN PYTHON FOR FINANCE: A GUIDE.: EXPLORING THE INTERSECTION OF FINANCE AND ML/AI: A PYTHON PRIMER Kindle Edition

by Dr Israel Carlos Lomovasky (Author)

-The Internet Of Minds (IOM). An Essay: The Future Implications of Brain Computer Interface

by Dr Israel Carlos Lomovasky (Author)

-CRYPTO TRADING TECHNICAL ANALYSIS: Apply the technical analysis indicators, time-frames and approaches that fit Crypto Currencies trading characteristics. Kindle Edition

by Dr Israel Carlos Lomovasky (Author)

-QUANTUM MACHINE LEARNING: A COMPREHENSIVE GUIDE WITH PRACTICAL EXAMPLES AND QUANTUM LANGUAGE IMPLEMENTATION: FROM BASICS TO ADVANCED.INCLUDES PYTHON CODE. (Quantum Computing Book 2) Kindle Edition

by Dr Israel Carlos Lomovasky (Author)

-CRYPTO BASICS TO ADVANCED. MAKE MONEY WITH CRYPTO.THE CRYPTO BUSINESS STARTUP BIBLE.: Investing ,trading and beyond. 20 Cryptocurrency profitable strategies. Over 100 startup ideas. Kindle Edition

by Dr Israel Carlos Lomovasky (Author)

-QUANTUM COMPUTING AND OPERATIONS RESEARCH.AN ESSAY.WHAT IS QC AND WHY IT MATTERS TO OR PRACTITIONERS.: THE FUTURE IMPLICATIONS OF QUANTUM COMPUTING ON OPTIMIZATION AND OPERATIONS RESEARCH. Kindle Edition

by Dr Israel Carlos Lomovasky (Author)

-ALGORITHMIC TRADING FROM SCRATCH TO AI/ML STRATEGIES IMPLEMENTED IN PYTHON.FOR CRYPTO,STOCKS,FOREX AND MORE.: RETAIL TRADING SYSTEMS FROM BASIC TO SOPHISTICATED STEP BY STEP. PYTHON FOR YOUR PROJECTS. Paperback – May 17, 2023

by Dr Israel Carlos Lomovasky (Author)

-CRYPTO SENTIMENT ALGO TRADING.PYTHON AND PSEUDO-CODE.: Algo Cryptocurrencies Trade: day, trend, news, swing, arbitrage, bots, contrarian, volume, event, seasonal ,and more strategies. Kindle Edition

by Dr Israel Carlos Lomovasky (Author)

-ALGORITHMIC TRADING STRATEGIES AND TECHNIQUES IN PYTHON, PSEUDO-CODE AND TRADESTATION CODE.: Get your projects started.20 most used techniques and strategies covering all tradeable assets. Kindle Edition

by Dr Israel Carlos Lomovasky (Author)

-ALGORITHMIC TRADING STRATEGIES AND TECHNIQUES IN PYTHON, PSEUDO-CODE AND TRADESTATION CODE.: Get your projects started.20 most used techniques and strategies covering all tradeable assets. Kindle Edition

by Dr Israel Carlos Lomovasky (Author)

-

www.ingramcontent.com/pod-product-compliance
Lightning Source LLC
LaVergne TN
LVHW022348060326
832902LV00022B/4319